Inuit Carvi
Far North

Inuits, called Eskimos by the 19th-century Europeans, are the original inhabitants of the Arctic tundra of northern Canada, Alaska, and Greenland. Inuit men still carve figures out of walrus ivory, caribou antlers, whale or seal bone, and soapstone. They carve natural figures such as animals, abstract shapes, and masks used for rituals and ceremonies.

Literature Connections:

Berry Woman's Children by Dale DeArmond; Greenwillow, 1985.
How Snowshoe Hare Rescued the Sun: A Tale from the Arctic by Emery & Durga Bernhard; Holiday House, 1993.
Thirty Indian Legends of Canada by Margaret Bemister; Firefly Books Ltd., 1991.
Whale Brother by Barbara Steiner; Walker & Co, 1988.

Make an Inuit Carving

▶ **Materials:**

- carving block made from plaster of Paris and vermiculite* (recipe follows)
- water
- one-half cup measuring scoop
- stir stick
- newspaper
- 1/2 gallon milk cartons (cut down)
- plastic bag
- carving tools (plastic spoon, nail)
- pattern on page 4
- spray varnish

▶ **Preparation:**

To make one carving block, mix
- 3 scoops of vermiculite* with
- 2 scoop plaster of Paris. Add about
- 2 scoops of water and stir
  until it looks like gravy.

Pour into the milk carton.
Let it sit for 1/2 hour. It will then be ready to carve.

(*vermiculite is a soil additive. It can be found in any store that sells plants and supplies.)

▶ **Steps to Follow:**

1. Working over newspaper, peel away the milk carton from the carving block.

2. Lay the pattern on the block and trace the outline with a pencil. Press hard enough to make the imprint of the pattern on the block.

3. Work all around the sides, scraping the plaster with a carving tool to shape it into a three dimensional figure.

   The body will have a block-like look, but it should have rounded edges and a form clearly recognizable from all sides.

4. If you run out of time, place your carving in a plastic bag. It will stay soft for two or three days.

   Remind students to imagine in their mind's eye what the finished sculpture will look like so they don't remove too much plaster.

   When the carving is complete and totally dry, protect it with a coat of spray varnish (sprayed outdoors by an adult).

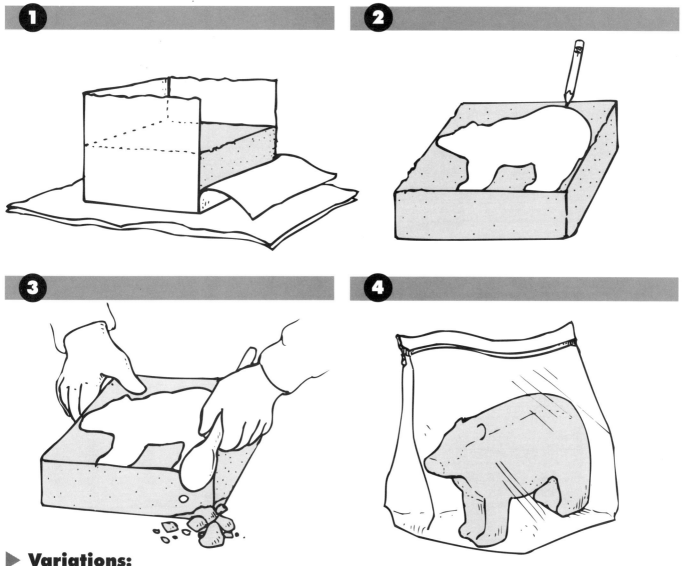

▶ Variations:

Instead of pouring the mixture into the milk carton, pour it into a plastic bag and treat it like clay. Wait until it starts to harden and then shape it (still in the bag) into the main shape of your carving.

Wait for half an hour. Remove the shape from the bag and carve the details you desire.

It can then be returned to the plastic bag to be worked on at a later time.

▶ Suggestions:

Label milk cartons with students' names. Carvings in progress should sit on a piece of paper labeled with student's name.

Let students draw their own animal to carve. Have them sketch the shape on a piece of paper first. Keep the shape simple. (How Snowshoe Hare Rescued the Sun, listed in Literature Connections on page 1, is an excellent source of animal shapes.)

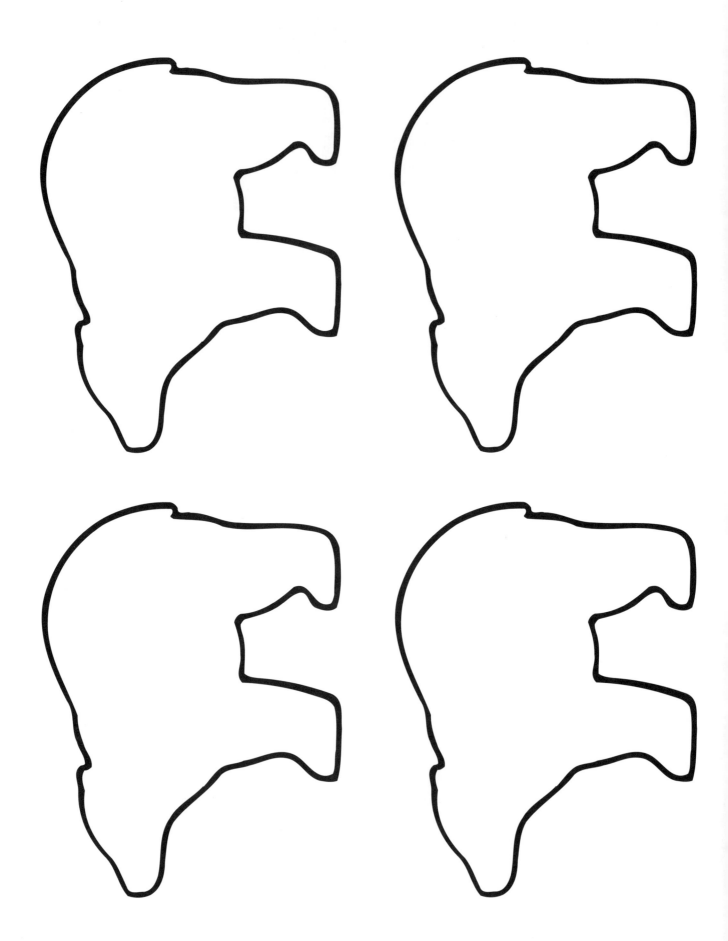

Northwest Coast Totem Poles
Far North

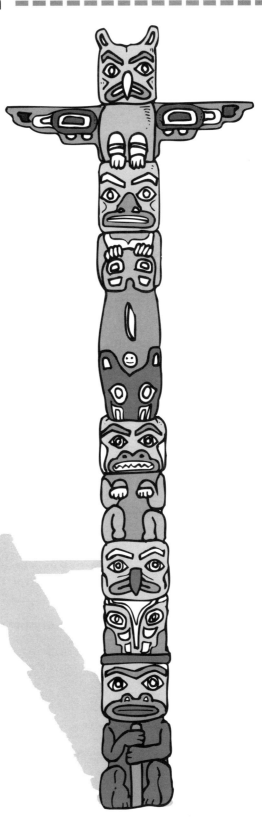

About 30 different tribes lived peacefully in the rainy Pacific Northwest almost untouched by Europeans until the late 1700s. They grew a little tobacco but never developed agriculture. The land, ocean, and rivers gave them everything they needed. They developed a complex hierarchal society and splendid works of art. Wealthy families, proud of their status, were able to display monumental art works, especially the towering wood totem poles. Each totem was different, and each carver tried to outdo his neighbor. The poles, when exposed to nature's elements, lasted about 60 years. New ones were carved to replace the old ones.

Literature Connections:

Once Upon a Totem by Christie Harris; Atheneum, 1973.
Talking Totem Poles by Glenn Holder; Dodd, Mead & Co., 1973.
Totem Pole by Diane Hoyt-Goldsmith; Holiday House, 1990.
Whale in the Sky by Anne Siberell; E. P. Dutton, 1982.

Make a Northwest Coast Totem Pole

▶ Materials:

- paper towel tube
- 4 inch (10 cm) square of corrugated cardboard
- patterns from pages 7 and 8
- scissors
- crayons or markers
- glue
- tape

▶ Preparation:

Collect the paper towel tubes well in advance.

Copy the patterns onto the heaviest paper or light weight tag board that you can. If this isn't possible, you can glue the photocopied patterns onto heavier paper, then cut them out.

▶ Steps to Follow:

1. At one end of the paper towel tube cut 1/2 inch (1 cm) slits every 1/4 inch (1/2 cm) all the way around the end.

2. Flare out the slits and set the tube on the cardboard square. Tape or glue the slits down securely. This will give the totem pole a base.

3. Color the patterns and cut them out.

4. Glue the patterns on the totem pole with the thunderbird on top.

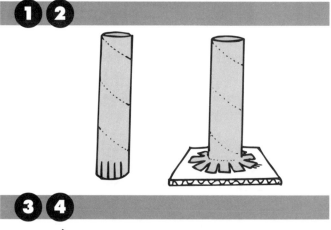

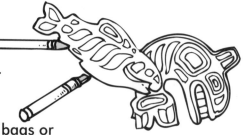

▶ Variations:

Have students create their own totem pole animals.

▶ Suggestions:

Student works in progress can be stored in zip-lock bags or brown paper bags with the students' names labeled on the outside.

Have students write a story about how the animals happened to be placed in that particular order on the totem pole.

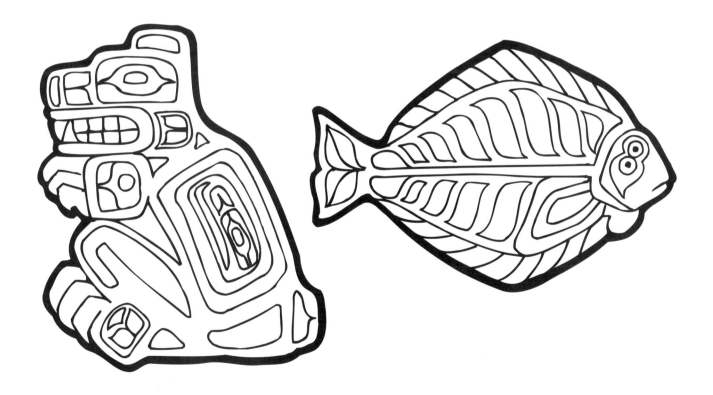

Folk Art Projects • North America EMC 724

Eskimo Mask
Far North

Eskimo masks are varied in design and purpose. Often they are carved from driftwood and made to seem larger by extending them with feathers. Three types of masks are made. Masks based on animals are made to aid hunters. The second type of mask, based on odd features of people, are used by performers in humorous plays. The third type of mask is made for the shaman, or medicine man. Eskimo masks are usually painted white or blue with red highlights.

Literature Connections:

Arctic Hunter by Diane Hoyt-Goldsmith; Holiday House, 1992.
Arctic Memories by Normee Ekooniak; Henry Holt & Co., 1988.
Masks Tell Stories by Carol Gelber; Millbrook Press, 1993.
They Put on Masks by Byrd Baylor; Charles Scribner, 1974.

Make an Eskimo Mask

▶ Materials:

- 1 salt dough recipe
- 9" x 12" (23 x 30.5 cm) piece of corrugated cardboard
- toothpicks
- tools for shaping (plastic knife and spoon)
- sandpaper
- glue
- tempera paints (white, blue, red)
- feathers

▶ Preparation:

Salt dough recipe:
- 1 cup salt
- 2 cups all-purpose flour
- 1 cup water
- 2-3 drops vegetable oil

Mix all the ingredients together. They may be stored in a plastic bag or used right away.

▶ Steps to Follow:

1. On top of the piece of cardboard (or any surface that can be moved to another place for drying), flatten most of the dough out into a rectangle that measures roughly 8 inches by 10 inches (20 cm x 25.5 cm). It should be about 1/2 to 1/4 inch (1-1/2 cm) thick. Save a little dough to add features.

2. Make thumb-print indentations in the rectangle for the eyes. Build up ridges around the indentations. Roll extra dough into eyeballs and set in the indentations.

   Add dough to shape a large nose that rises up from the face. Roll extra dough into balls and place in the nostrils.

3. Shape a large open mouth. Have lips open and rising above the face. Use extra dough to form large teeth.

4. Using the toothpick, poke holes around the outer edge of the mask so you can later glue in feathers.

   Let clay dry thoroughly. You can sun-dry the pieces or bake them at 200°F (93°C) for about two hours or bake overnight with oven door ajar. Do not use higher temperature or pieces will turn brown and crack.

   Sand dried pieces to remove rough spots.

5. Paint your mask with tempera paint.

   Decorate the outer edge of the mask by gluing feathers into the holes made by the toothpick.

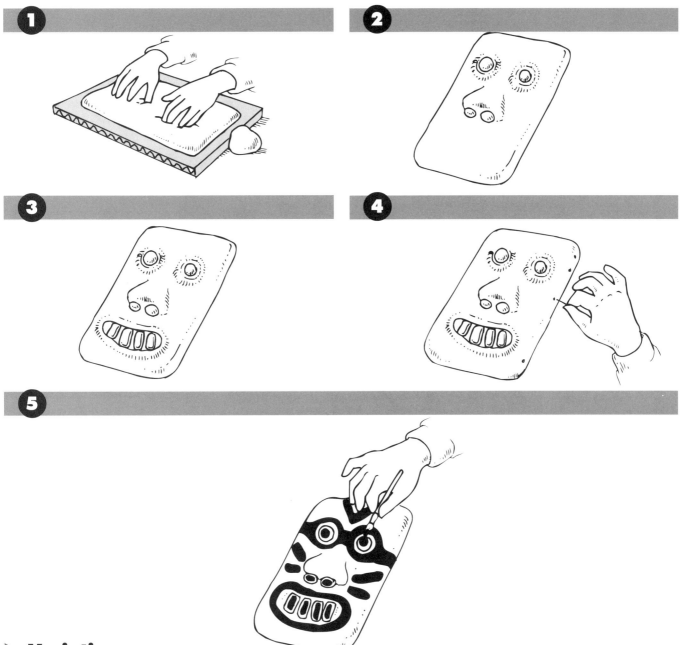

▶ Variations:

The mask may also be decorated with any item found in nature: small sticks, acorns, shells, seed pods, etc.

The mask may be sprayed with a matte or glossy varnish before gluing on the feathers.

▶ Suggestions:

If your dough is sticky, spread a little flour on your work area.

The mask described here is only an example. Encourage students to design their own masks after studying the Eskimo culture. You may wish to make an overhead transparency of the masks on page 12 to point out styles and features.

 Folk Art Projects • North America EMC 724

Note: If students design their own masks (see page 11, last paragraph) these samples may provide guidance.

Chilkat Blanket
Far North

The women of the Tlingit tribes wove hair from the wild mountain goat with cedar bark to make beautiful Chilkat blankets. Only people of rank or wealthy people owned them. The blankets were so highly regarded that other tribes eagerly traded their valuables for the chance to own one. It took about a year to design the pattern; make, dye, and dry the yarn; and weave the blanket. Designs represented parts of fish, birds, or animals and were always symmetrical. The blanket was woven in shades of yellow, blue, black, and off white. It was trimmed with long fringe at the bottom.

Literature Connections:

Clamshell Boy: A Makah Legend by Terri Cohlene; Rourke, 1990.
Northern Lullaby by Nancy White Carlstrom; Philomel, 1992.
Raven's Light: A Myth from the People of the Northwest Coast retold by Susan Hand Shetterly; Atheneum, 1991.
Raven: A Trickster Tale from the Pacific Northwest told by Gerald McDermott; Harcourt Brace Jovanovich, 1993.

Make a Chilkat Blanket

▶ Materials:

- pattern on pages 15-16
- crayons or markers
- scissors
- hole punch
- glue
- 18 pieces of white or off-white yarn each 12" (30.5 cm) long

▶ Preparation:

Discuss with class what a mirror image is. Explain how a Chilkat blanket is prepared. Explain that if the blanket were folded in half down the middle, the two halves would be identical.

▶ Steps to Follow:

1. Carefully cut out the two pattern pieces.

2. Apply glue to the glue strip of the right pattern piece. Lay the left-hand piece on top of the strip lining up the pattern exactly. Press firmly in place.

3. Color the blanket yellow, blue, black, leaving some spaces white or coloring them off-white. Be careful to color correctly. The pattern should be colored so that it is symmetrical. Using a hole punch, punch out the holes along the bottom of the blanket.

4. Take one piece of yarn, fold it in half, poke the folded end through a hole, and slip the loose ends through the loop. Pull gently.

   Continue until the entire lower edge has a fringe hanging down.

▶ Suggestions:

Older students can design their own chilkat blanket. Have them design half the blanket, then place a mirror along the edge to see what the entire blanket would look like.

Students can then exchange their halves. The goal would be to complete the design.

14

Folk Art Projects • North America EMC 724

Apply Glue Here

Folk Art Projects • North America EMC 724

Apple Head Figures
Americana

The first apple trees in America were planted in Massachusetts a few years after the Pilgrims arrived. Because the apple was so delicious and could be used in a variety of ways, orchards were planted in every settlement. And, because they could be dried to keep for long periods of time, they were soon used to create apple head faces, sometimes called "Granny Dolls."

Literature Connections:

The Amazing Apple Book by Paulette Bourgeois; Addison-Wesley, 1987.
Johnny Appleseed: A Tall Tale by Steven Kellogg; Morrow Junior Books, 1988.
The Life and Times of the Apple by Charles Micucci; Orchard Books, 1992.
The Seasons of Arnold's Apple Tree by Gail Gibbons; Harcourt Brace Jovanovich, 1984.

Make an Apple Head Scarecrow

▶ Materials:

For head:
- 1 small to medium sized apple
  (preferably with a stem)
  (Buy inexpensive bulk-bagged apples.)
- potato peeler or small knife
- 12" (30.5 cm) thread or string
- safe carving utensils
  (spoons, nails, tweezers, blunt knives, etc.)
- bottled lemon juice
  (if you don't want your head to turn brown)
- newspaper
- dried beans, rice, cotton, fiber fill, etc.
  to decorate head
- white glue
- glue gun

For body:
- 8" (20 cm) dowel or chopstick
- 2 8" (20 cm) squares of burlap
  or similar coarse material
- 2-3" pieces of straw or broomstraw
- twine
- pattern on page 20

▶ Directions for making the head:

1. Peel the apple with a potato peeler or small knife, leaving the stem and a small circle of peel around the stem.

2. Carve a mouth, eyes, and nose. Keep the cuts simple but fairly deep. After carving, soak the head in a bowl of bottled lemon juice for one hour. This will keep the apple from turning brown. You may skip this step if you are going for the "aged" look.

3. Tie the thread or string to the stem of the apple. If the apple does not have a stem, use a large paper clip. Straighten most of the clip, leaving one end bent as a hook and attach the string. Push the straightened end all the way through the core. Fold a piece of masking tape over the hanging string. Write the student's name or initials on the tape.

4. The head can be completed using a variety of materials. Dried beans can be glued in the eyeholes. Rice can serve as teeth. Cotton or fiber fill can serve as hair.

   Folk Art Projects • North America EMC 724

1

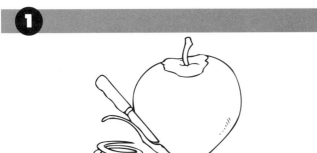

2

3

Hang heads in a warm, dry place where they will not be disturbed for at least 3 weeks.

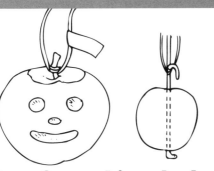

4

▶ Directions for making the body:

1. Push an 8 inch (20 cm) dowel, chopstick, or similar stick into the bottom of the completed head. Pull the stick out, apply hot glue to the end of the stick and push back in.

2. Using the pattern on page 20, cut 2 pieces from burlap. Pull threads out of the ends of the arms and legs to give it a "ragged" look.

3. Using white glue, glue the two pieces of burlap together with the stick in between. Before gluing the arm and leg openings closed, put in pieces of straw or broom straw and let it stick out the openings.

4. If desired, a scrap of burlap can be added for a hat. Twine can be tied around the waist.

1

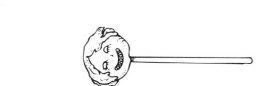

2

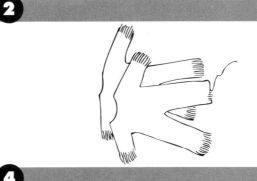

3

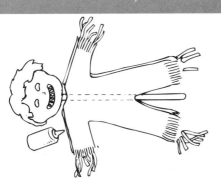

4

 Folk Art Projects • North America EMC 724

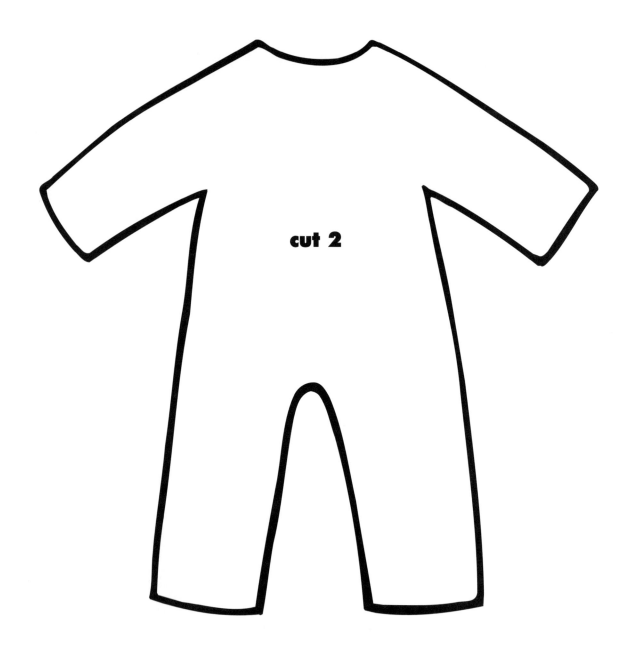

cut 2

Appalachian Buttonhole Puzzle
Americana

Handmade puzzles were once a favorite pastime for children and grown-ups in America. Although the origin of these puzzles can be traced to other countries, we give credit to the inventive people of the southern Appalachian mountain region for what we now call American folk toys. These people changed and improved many traditional hand puzzles as well as inventing their own. Puzzles have taken on new names according to their appearance, method of working, or theme.

Literature Connections:

ABC Americana by Cynthia Rubin; Harcourt Brace Jovanovich, 1989.
Billy's Button by William Accorsi; Greenwillow, 1992.
Careers in Toy Making by Mark Lerner; Lerner Publications, 1980.
Cat's Cradle, Owl's Eyes: A Book of String Games by Camilla Gryski; Morrow, 1984.
School's Out: Puzzles That Take You Cool Places by Chiu; Bantam, 1995.

Make a Buttonhole Puzzle

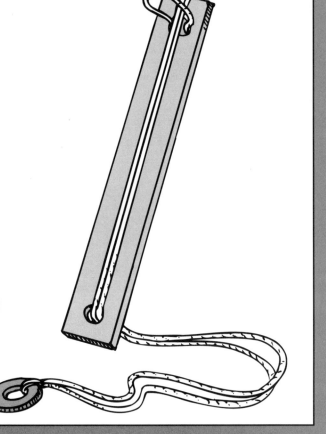

▶ Materials:

- tongue depressor
- scissors
- 42" (106.5 cm) piece of nylon cord or polyester twine
- 1 large stringing bead, ring, or washer
- electric drill

▶ Preparation:

Cut the rounded ends off the tongue depressor to make squared ends.
To drill holes in the tongue depressors, masking tape about 6 of them together and drill the largest possible hole in each end.

▶ Directions for Making Buttonhole Puzzle:

1. Fold the 42" (106.5 cm) string in half.

   Push the folded end of the string through a hole in the tongue depressor.

2. Bring the two ends of the string over the top of the stick and through the loop and pull until it is snug.

3. Weave the two ends through the other hole as shown. Loosely tie both string ends to the bead, string, or washer. (After solving the puzzle, you will need to untie the bead, etc. to set up the puzzle again.)

   The bead must be large enough so that it will not pass through the holes.

   The object of the puzzle is to remove the string with the attached bead through the "buttonholes" without cutting or untying the string.

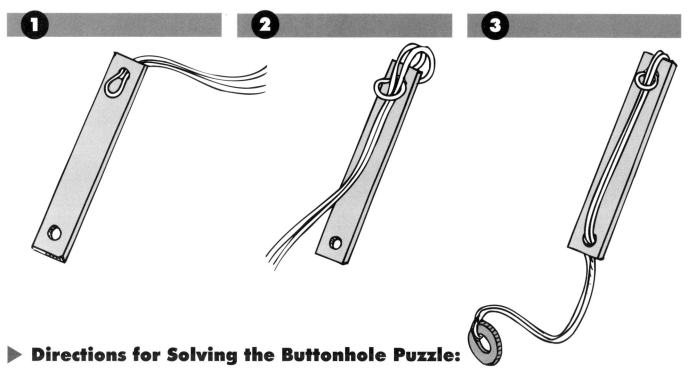

▶ Directions for Solving the Buttonhole Puzzle:

1. Grab the loop and pull it down and through the bottom hole.

2. Spread the loop and bring it up and over the top of the wood strip. Let the loop drop behind the wood strip.

3. Pull the ring down by tugging repeatedly; the string will separate from the wood strip. Untie the washer and set up the puzzle for the next person to solve.

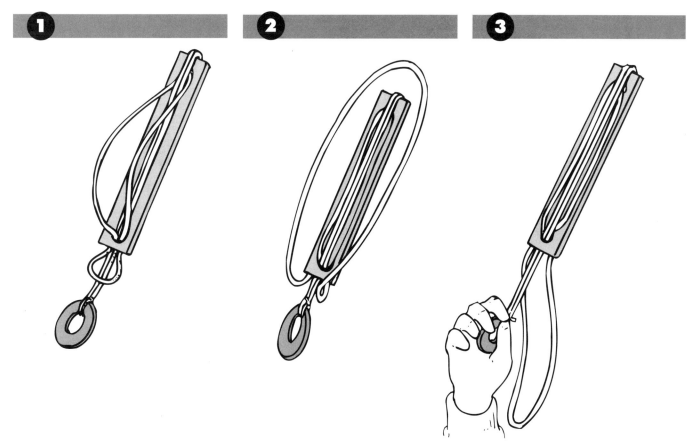

Tin Lantern
------ Americana ------

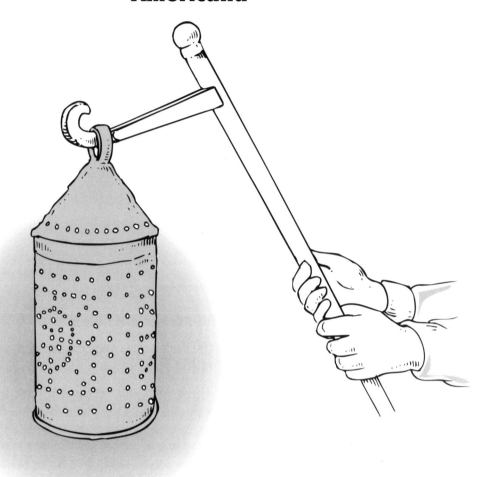

In Early America the tin lantern was used for carrying a lit candle from place to place. Fires were not easy to start, and it was very important to "keep" a flame once you had it going. Glass lanterns were rare and very expensive. Tin was inexpensive and looked almost like silver when it was new and shiny. A pattern of small holes was punched in the tin, creating an object that was decorative as well as functional.

Literature Connections:

Daily Life: A Sourcebook on Colonial America from the series American Albums from the Collections of the Library of Congress; Millbrook, 1991.
Kate Shelley and the Midnight Express by Margaret Wetterer; Carolrhoda Books, 1990.
Keep the Lights Burning, Abbie by Peter and Connie Roop; Carolrhoda Books, 1985.

Make a Tin Lantern

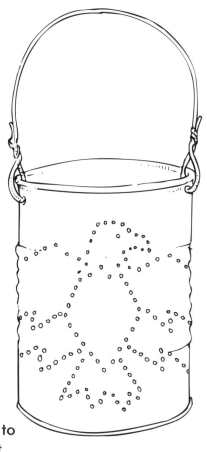

▶ Materials:

- tin can (a one-pound coffee can size is best)
- patterns on page 27
- permanent marker
- water
- different sized nails
- hammer
- several layers of newspaper or a folded towel
- light weight wire
- wire cutters
- candle

▶ Preparation:

Remove all labels from the can. Remove the top; retain the bottom.

Before the holes can be punched, the can needs to be filled with water and the water frozen. This provides a more stable surface for hammering the nails.

You may need to make arrangements for this if you do not have access to a freezer at school. Elicit help from parents who live close to school. You may only be able to have a small group of students at a time do this project.

▶ Steps to Follow:

1. Remove the can from the freezer. Tape the pattern to the can.

2. Place the can on several layers of newspaper or on a folded towel.

   Using a hammer and nail, hammer holes through the points on the pattern and into the can. Vary the size of holes by using different sized nails.

   Remove the pattern.

3. Make holes for a handle on opposite sides of the can rim.

   Set the can in a sink or tub so the ice can melt, or place the can under running water until the ice pulls away from the sides of the can. Discard the ice.

4. Cut wire a desired length for a handle. Wind through holes at can rim.

   Drip wax from a candle into the bottom of the lantern and mount the candle standing straight up.

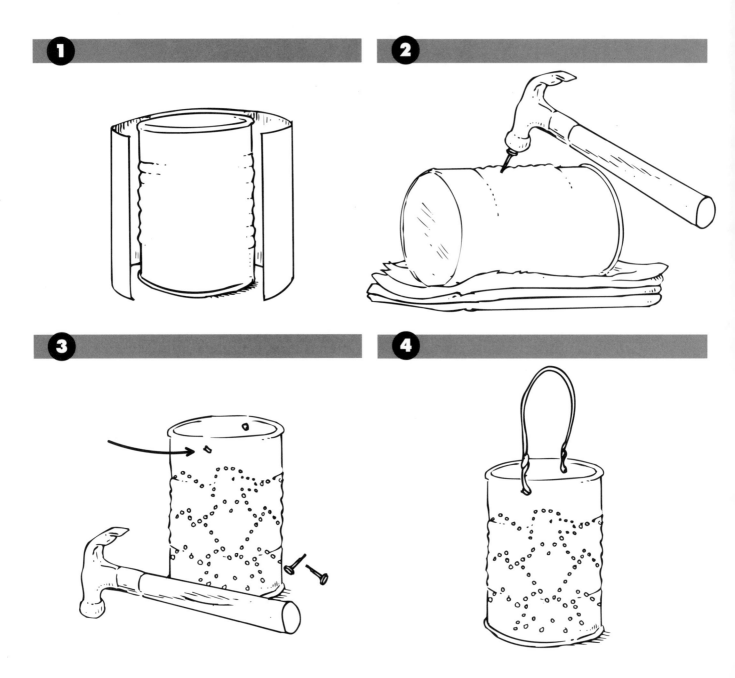

▶ Suggestions:

• Let students design their own pattern around a patriotic theme.
• Students may choose to randomly punch holes creating a swirling or abstract effect.
• Make Dipped Candles (page 28) to use in your tin lanterns.

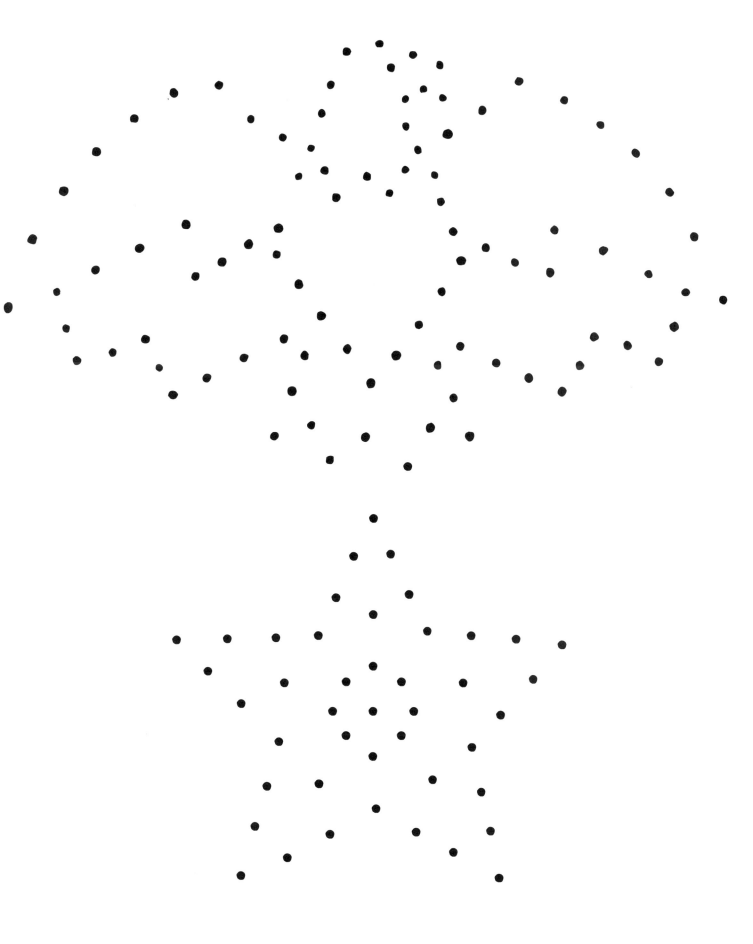

Folk Art Projects • North America EMC 724

Dipped Candles
Americana

In Colonial America candles were used for lighting homes before the invention of gas and electric lamps. It took a whole cluster of candles to be able to read and write. Only rich families were able to light their homes brightly after the sun went down because candles were hard to make and expensive to buy. Using the dip process, even an expert candle maker could only make about 100 candles a day.

Literature Connections:

Candlemaking Design Book by Carol Feder; Watts, 1974.
Candle Tales by Julia Cunningham; Pantheon Books, 1964.
A Pioneer Sampler: The Daily Life of a Pioneer Family in 1840 by Barbara Greenwood; Ticknor & Fields, 1995.
Pioneer Voices; Our First Year in the New World by Connie and Peter Roop; Walker, 1995.

Make Dipped Candles

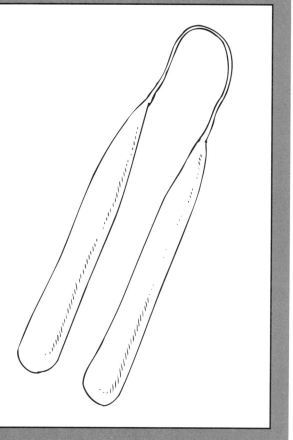

▶ Materials:

- paraffin wax
  (can be purchased in craft or grocery stores)
- cotton string or wicking material
  (can be purchased in craft stores)
- large cooking pot
- tall tin can that can fit comfortably in
  the cooking pot (large coffee can)
- fork
- scissors
- source of heat: stove top, hot plate, etc.
- newspaper

▶ Preparation:

Candle dipping can be messy. Spread
newspaper around the work area.

Make sure an adult is available to supervise
at all times.

▶ Steps to Follow:

1. Fill the tall tin can about two-thirds full of
   water and place it in the cooking pot.

   Fill the pot half full with water and put it
   over medium heat.

2. As the water in the pot begins to boil, add
   chunks of paraffin to the can until it is
   almost full. Wax is lighter than water and
   will float. This way the paraffin is used
   much more economically. For candle
   dipping, the wax must be at just the right
   temperature. Test with a sample wick. If it is
   too hot, the wax will slide off the wick. If it
   is too cool, it will be too thick.

3. Cut a piece of string at least twice as
   long as the can height. Weave the string
   between the tines of a fork, making
   sure the same amount hangs down on
   either side.

4. Holding the fork handle, dip the dangling
   string ends into the can until they touch the
   bottom. Pull the wicks up and let them cool.

   Continue to dip, always letting the wax
   harden between dippings, until the candles
   are the thickness you desire.

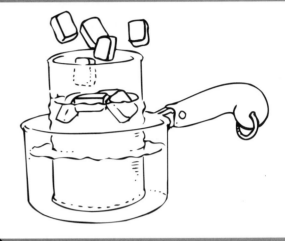

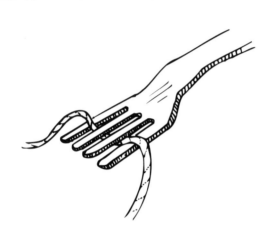

▶ Suggestions:

You may hurry along the process of cooling the dipped candles by having a tall pitcher with cold water handy. Pull the candles from the wax and dip them in the cold water to cool them off quickly.

When the candles are complete they will be connected as was typical of all dipped candles in Early America.

Cut the loop and trim the wick to about a half-inch long.

The candles would look wonderful in a tin lantern (see page 24).

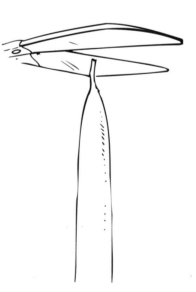

Jacob's Ladder
Americana

Spirituals are emotional, religious folk songs. Created by enslaved African Americans, spirituals are a combination of African musical traditions and religious songs of the 19th century white South. "Climbing Jacob's Ladder" is a spiritual based on the biblical story of a man named Jacob who dreamed he saw angels traveling up and down a ladder reaching to heaven. The wooden toy is designed to mimic a moving staircase.

Literature Connections:

All Night, All Day: A Child's First Book of African-American Spirituals selected by Ashley Bryan; Atheneum, 1991.
I'm Going To Sing: Black American Spirituals, Volume Two selected by Ashley Bryan; Atheneum, 1982.
Praise for the Singing by Madelaine Gill; Little, Brown & Co., 1993
Spin a Soft Black Song by Nikki Giovanni; Farrar, Straus & Giroux, 1985.
Games by Caroline Pitcher; Watts, 1984.

Make Jacob's Ladder

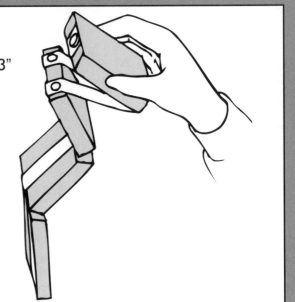

▶ **Materials:**

- 4 equal-sized blocks of wood, each 2 1/2" to 3" (6 to 7.5 cm) square and 1/2" (1 cm) thick
- fine sandpaper
- 3 pieces of narrow ribbon each 14" (35.5 cm) long
- scissors
- hammer
- 12 flat head thumbtacks

▶ **Preparation:**

Finely sand all sides of the 4 blocks of wood.

▶ **Steps to Follow:**

1. Using the hammer and two tacks, gently tack two of the ribbons to the end of one of the wood blocks about one fourth of the way in from each side. Lay the ribbons across the block.

2. Turn the wood block so the tacks are facing away from you and the ribbons are coming toward you.

   Tack the third piece of ribbon to the edge of the wood block facing you between the first two ribbons. Lay that ribbon across the block away from you.

3. Place another wood block on top, with the ribbons in the middle and their tails hanging out.

   Fold the middle ribbon over the top block. Pull it tight and tack it to the end edge of the block farthest from you.

4. Pull up the other 2 ribbons and tack them to the end edge of the top block closest to you.

5. Put the 3rd block on top, sandwiching all 3 ribbons in between blocks 2 and 3. Pull up the middle ribbon and tack it to the end edge closest to you.

6. Pull the two outer ribbons up over the top of the block. Tack them to the end edge farthest from you.

7. Place the 4th block on top. Make sure all 3 ribbons are between the top 2 blocks.

   Pull the middle ribbon up over the top of the block. Tack it on the end farthest from you.

8. Pull up the 2 outer ribbons and tack them to the end closest to you. Trim the extra from all 3 ribbons.

   To play with your Jacob's Ladder, pick up the top block by its edges. Tilt the block until it touches the second block. The block will look as if it's tumbling down.

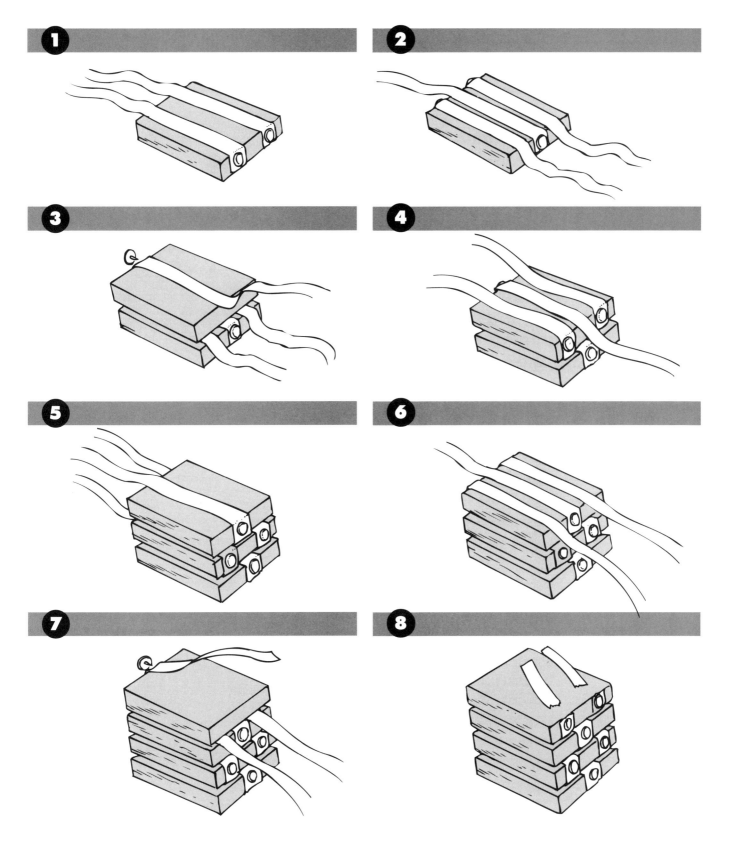

▶ Suggestions:

Enlist parent help for all age groups. This project requires extra effort, but it is worth it.

Pennsylvania Dutch Barn Sign
Americana

In parts of Pennsylvania, Virginia, and West Virginia, barns were, and still are, decorated with signs. The Amish and Mennonites who settled in southern Pennsylvania in the 17th century are given credit for starting the tradition. The colorful signs were once thought to be good luck symbols that would ward off sickness, fire, lightning, and bad luck. Today they are used for decoration. Typical designs include stars with up to thirty-two points. They are painted in yellow, white, red, and black. The star symbols have different meanings depending on the number of points.

---

4 points - good luck
5 points - good health, protection from lightning
double five-pointed star - good weather
6 points - love and good marriage
7 points - wards off evil
8 points - good will, land ownership
12 points - wisdom and sincerity
16 points - justice

Literature Connections:

Appalachia: The Voices of Sleeping Birds by Cynthia Rylant; Harcourt, 1991.
The Folks In the Valley: A Pennsylvania Dutch ABC by Jim Aylesworth; HarperCollins, 1992.
Just Plain Fancy by Patricia Polaco; Bantam, 1990.
Where Time Stands Still by Sally Foster; Dodd, Mead & Co., 1987.

Make a Pennsylvania Dutch Barn Sign

▶ Materials:

- drawing paper
- circle template on page 36
- barn sign designs on pages 37, 38, 39
- pencil
- ruler
- yellow, white, red, and black crayons or markers

▶ Preparation:

Determine the option you wish students to use:

1. Young students can color the patterns.

2. Older students can create a barn design using the circle template. Make overhead transparencies of the barn sign designs. Use these to talk about the nature of barn designs with your students. Then follow the steps below.

▶ Steps to Follow:

1. Using a pencil and ruler, students can recreate one of the sample barn designs or make a geometric design of their own.

   Demonstrate how to make evenly spaced points within the circle:
   - with a pencil and ruler, draw evenly spaced spokes between the larger inner circle and the smaller outer circle.
   - on the larger inside circle make a dot halfway between each spoke. Draw lines from the outer tips of the spokes to the dots. This will make the star points.

2. Color brightly.

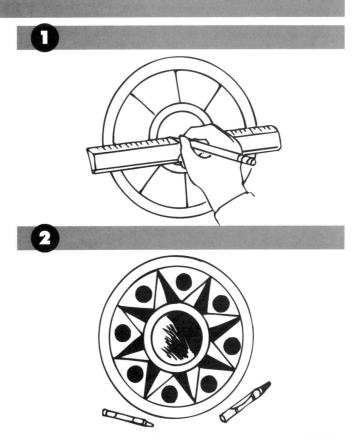

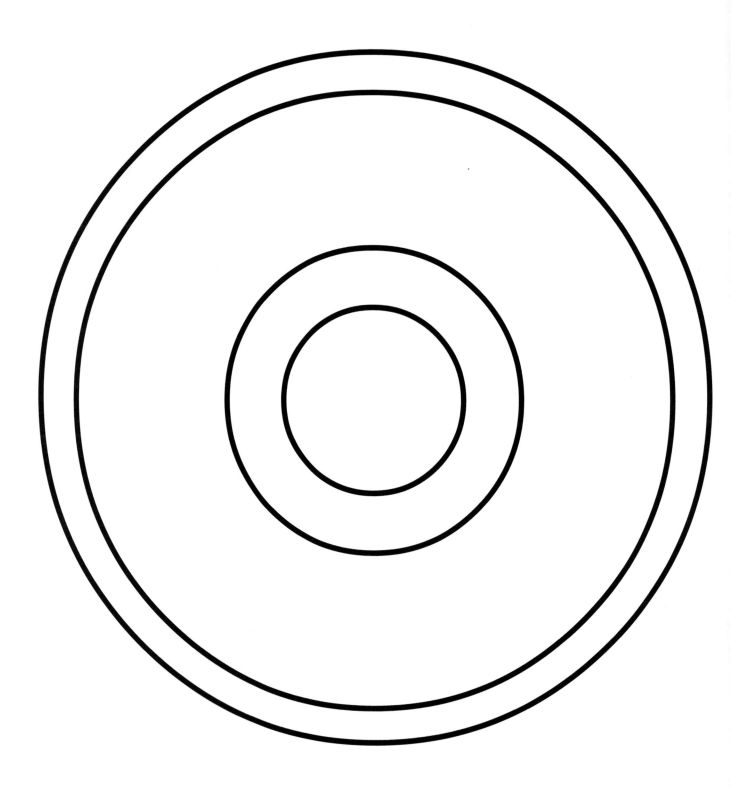

36 Folk Art Projects • North America EMC 724

37

Folk Art Projects • North America EMC 724

Folk Art Projects • North America EMC 724

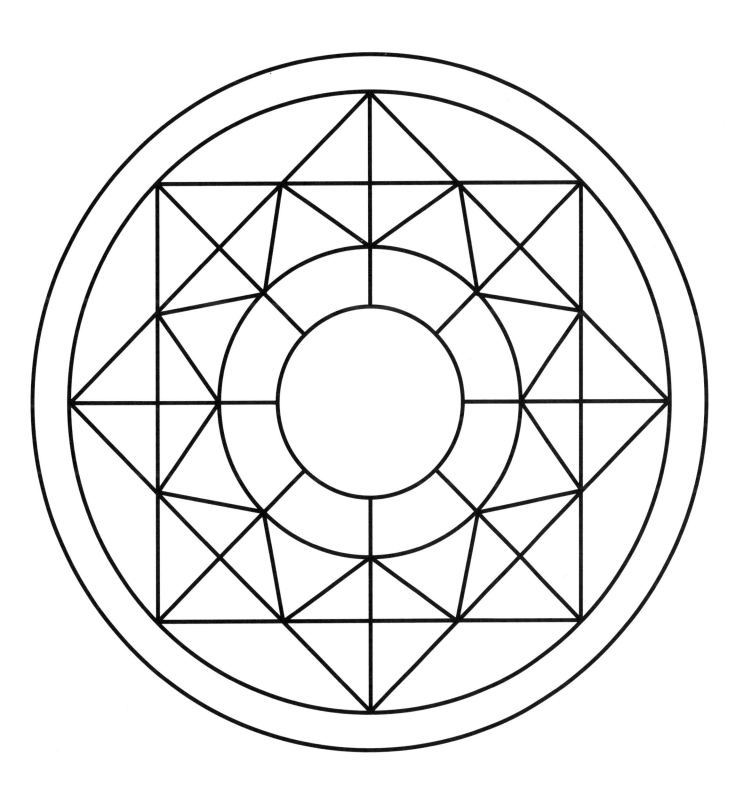

Folk Art Projects • North America EMC 724

Kachina Doll
Native American

Kachina is a Hopi word with three meanings. First, it means a god or spirit. It is also used to name masked dancers impersonating these spirits. Third, it stands for small painted dolls. These dolls were made for the children of the tribe so they might become familiar with the legends and the roles of many of the kachinas (gods). They are not toys, but an important part of a Pueblo child's education. There are hundreds of kachinas or spirits in the form of animals, birds, places, or people. Some kachinas are pictured as ogres who frighten children into obedience to their parents.

Literature Connections:

Children of the Earth and Sky: Five Stories About Native American Children by Stephen Krensky; Scholastic, 1992.
The Day of the Ogre Kachinas by Janet Hammond; Holt, Rinehart, Winston, 1994.
Kachina Dolls: An Educational Coloring Book by Linda Spizzirri; Spizzirri Publishing, 1982.
Warrior Maiden: A Hopi Legend by Ellen Schecter; Bantam, 1992.

Make a Kachina Doll

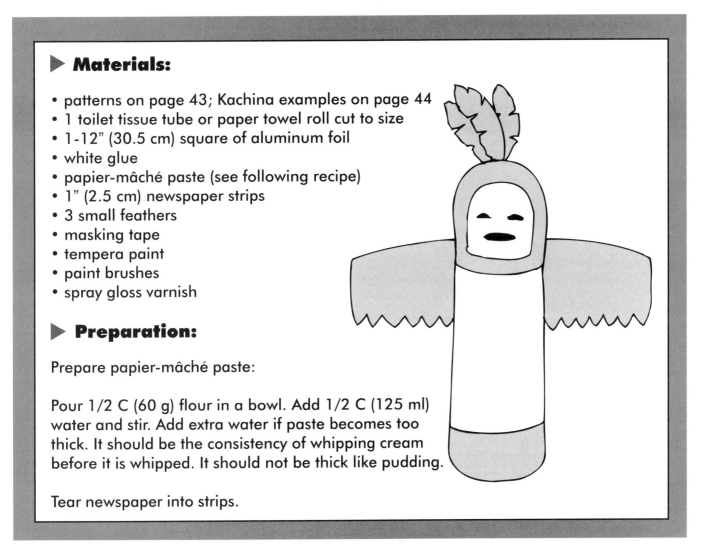

▶ **Materials:**

- patterns on page 43; Kachina examples on page 44
- 1 toilet tissue tube or paper towel roll cut to size
- 1-12" (30.5 cm) square of aluminum foil
- white glue
- papier-mâché paste (see following recipe)
- 1" (2.5 cm) newspaper strips
- 3 small feathers
- masking tape
- tempera paint
- paint brushes
- spray gloss varnish

▶ **Preparation:**

Prepare papier-mâché paste:

Pour 1/2 C (60 g) flour in a bowl. Add 1/2 C (125 ml) water and stir. Add extra water if paste becomes too thick. It should be the consistency of whipping cream before it is whipped. It should not be thick like pudding.

Tear newspaper into strips.

▶ **Steps to Follow:**

1. Loosely roll the sheet of aluminum foil into a ball. Tape it to the top of the toilet tissue roll.

2. Dip the newspaper strips one at a time in the paste. Hold each strip with one hand and remove excess paste with the fingers of the other hand.

   Apply the newspaper strips and paper mâché paste in a single layer completely covering the ball and tube.

   Apply strips in various directions, overlapping as necessary. Let this dry completely before painting.

3. Cut wings, horns, arms or other distinguishing characteristics from tag board or old file folders. Attach on the back with glue.

4. Paint the hair dark. Leave the face light. Add a simple mouth and eyes.

   Paint the body as desired.

5. Lay the feathers on the sticky side of a 3 inch (7.5 cm) piece of masking tape. Attach the tape to the back of the doll's head.

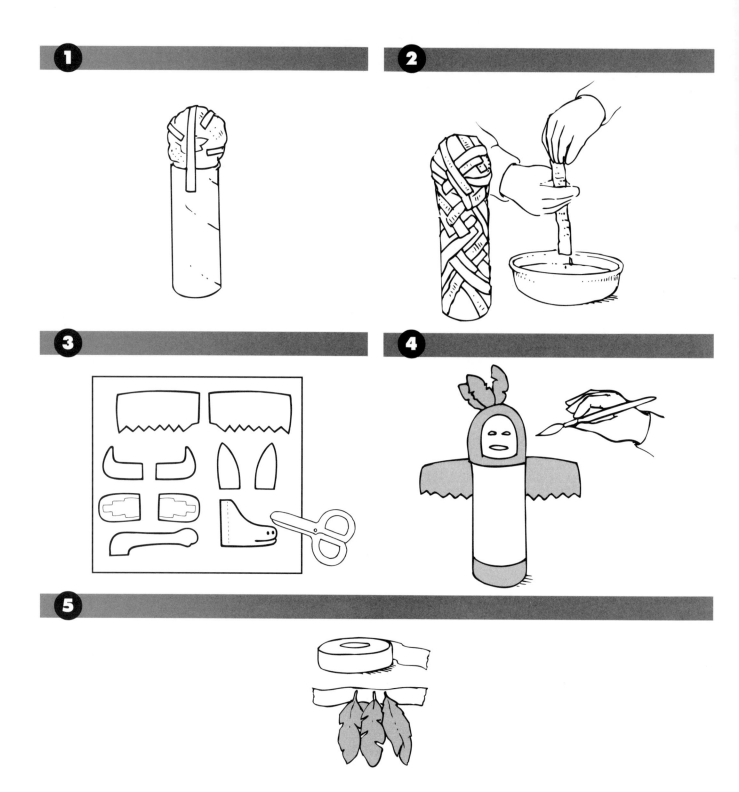

▶ Variation:

Let students choose the animal, bird or person they want to represent. Let them come up with the characteristics that should be displayed.

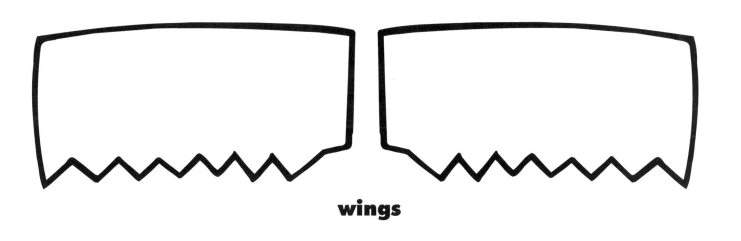

wings

Optional patterns—see variation, page 42

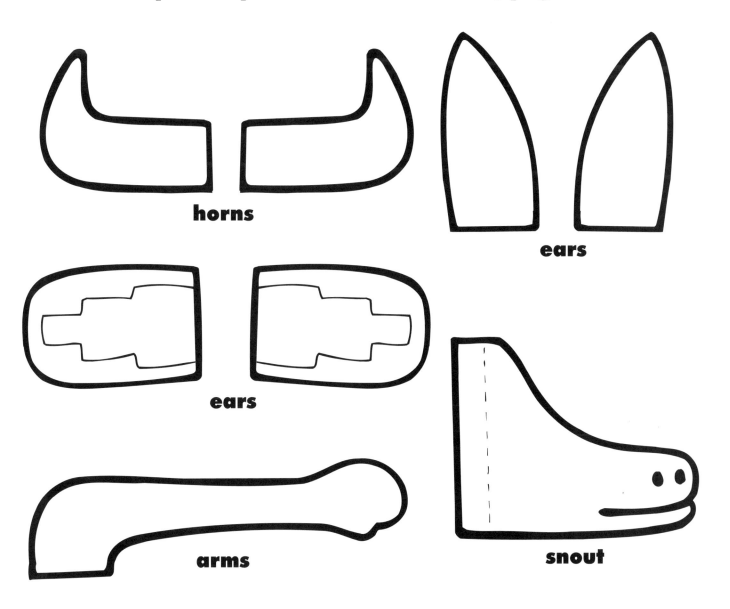

horns

ears

ears

arms

snout

Folk Art Projects • North America EMC 724

Kachina Dolls

 Folk Art Projects • North America EMC 724

Sun Dance Buffalo Skull Mask
Native American

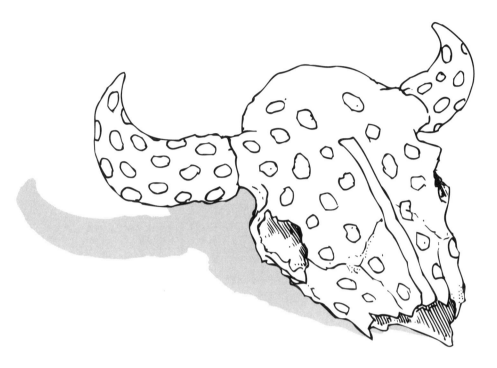

The Plains Indians held the Sun Dance, the greatest of their ceremonies, at the time of the summer buffalo hunt. The ceremony differed from tribe to tribe, but the purpose was the same: to thank the Great Spirit for past help and pray for future blessings. The ceremony lasted several days and nights. Because the buffalo was a vital resource to their way of life, most Plains people painted buffalo skulls and decorated them with sage and grass. These played a prominent part in the ceremony.

Literature Connections:

Buffalo by Emilie U. Lepthien; Children's Press, 1989.
Buffalo Dance: A Blackfoot Legend by Nancy Van Laan; Little, Brown & Co., 1993.
Buffalo Sunrise: The Story of a North American Giant by Diane Swanson; Sierra Club, 1996.
Buffalo Woman by Paul Goble; Bradbury, 1984.
Great Buffalo Race: How the Buffalo Got Its Hump: A Seneca Tale by Helen K. David; Little, Brown & Co., 1994.
North American Indian Masks by Frieda Gates: Walker, 1982.
Where the Buffaloes Begin by Olaf Baker; Puffin Books, 1985.

Make a Buffalo Skull Mask

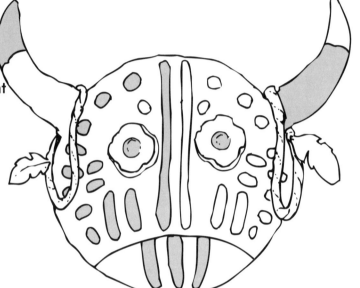

▶ Materials:

- mask example on page 48
- white, 9" (23 cm) heavy duty paper plate
- papier mâché paste
- newspaper strips
- 2 egg cups from an egg carton
- 2 12" (30.5 cm) squares of
  aluminum foil
- white, black, and red tempera paint
- paintbrush
- masking tape
- scissors
- stapler
- yarn pieces
- 2 feathers

▶ Preparation:

Prepare papier mâché paste:

Pour 1/2 C (60 g) flour in a bowl. Add 1/2 C (125 ml) water and stir. Add extra water if paste becomes too thick. It should be the consistency of whipping cream before it is whipped. It should not be thick like pudding.

Tear newspaper into strips.

▶ Steps to Follow:

1. Cut two 3 inch (7.5 cm) slits into the edge of the paper plate about 4 inches (10 cm) apart. Angle the cuts slightly so that they are closer together toward the center than on the edge.

2. Overlap the edges of the cuts and staple them closed. This bends the plate in the middle to give it the appearance of a nose.

3. Tape on the two egg carton sections for the eye sockets.

4. Form the horns by crumpling the aluminum foil into tube-like shapes, tapering them at the ends. The two pieces should be about 8 inches (20 cm) long and curved in at the top. Staple horns to each side of the paper plate at the top, attaching them from behind the plate.

5. Loosely wad up newspaper under the plate for support while you apply layers of paper mâché.

Dip the newspaper strips one at a time in the paste. Hold each strip with one hand and remove excess paste with the fingers of the other hand.

Apply strips in various directions, overlapping as necessary. Cover the complete skull and horns, except for the tops of the egg carton sections, with a single layer. Let this layer dry completely. Apply a second coat of papier mâché.

6. Let this coat dry completely. Paint the entire skull with two coats of white paint.

Paint one horn black with a red tip and the other red with a black tip.

Paint the eyes black.

Paint half the face with red dots and stripes and the other half with black dots and stripes.

Paint the mouth area red with black stripes.

The black paint symbolized the earth and the red symbolized the people. The dots symbolized their prayers.

7. Tie each feather to a loop of yarn and hang one over each horn.

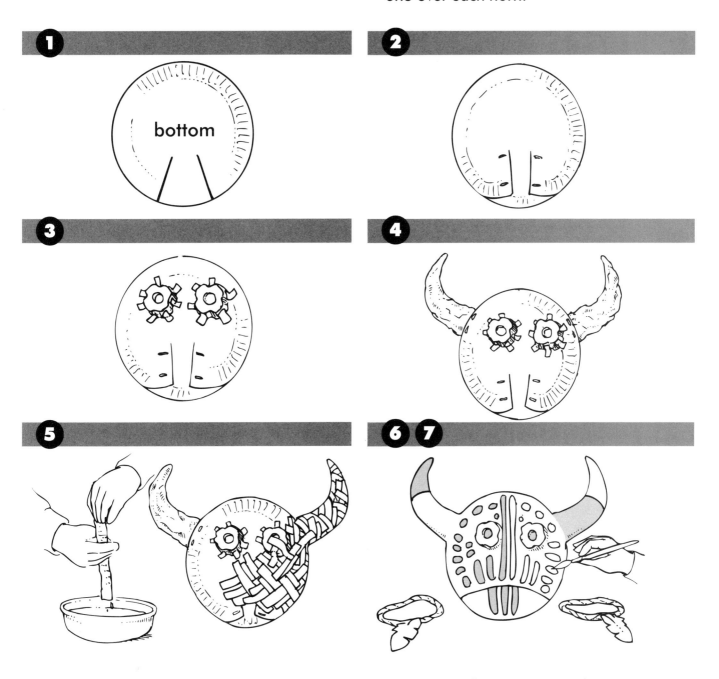

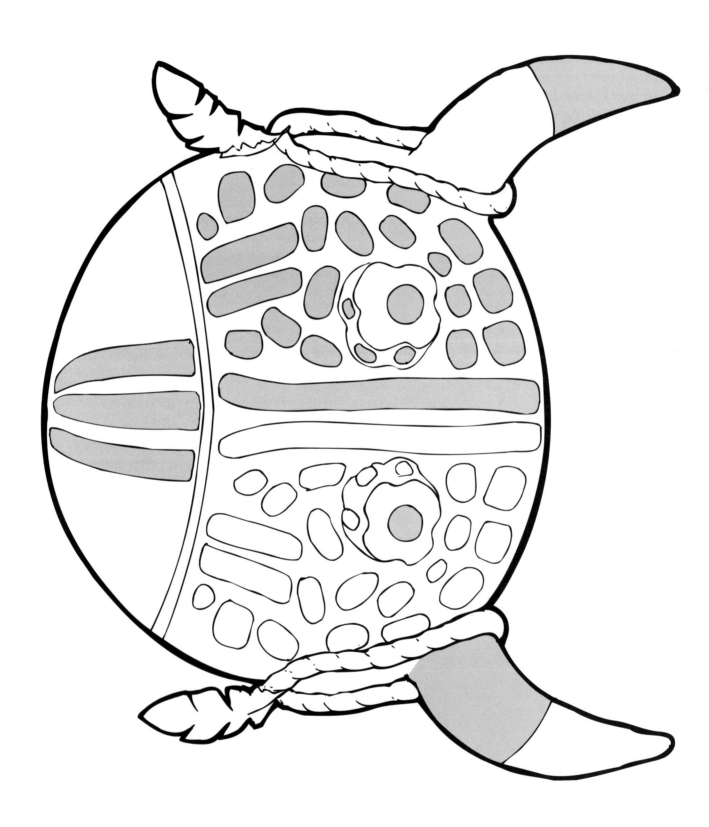

Cornhusk Dolls
Native American

South American and Central American Indian children and their North American neighbors all played with cornhusk dolls. Colonial mothers who made cornhusk toys for their children continued the tradition of one of the oldest known toys. Cornhusk dolls are still made in the Ozark Mountains of Missouri and the Southern Appalachians.

Literature Connections:

Corn Is Maize: The Gift of the Indians by Aliki; Crowell, 1976.
Indian Corn and Other Gifts by Sigmund Lavine; Dodd, Mead & Co., 1974.
People of the Corn: A Mayan Story retold by Mary-Joan Gerson; Little, Brown & Co., 1995.
Three Stalks of Corn by Leo Politi; Charles Scribner, 1976.

Make a Cornhusk Doll

▶ Materials:

- 6-8 dried cornhusks (they can be purchased in the Mexican food or produce section of grocery stores or in craft stores)
- scissors
- newspapers

▶ Preparation:

Soak cornhusks in water overnight.

The next day tear narrow strips off one cornhusk to use for tying.

Spread husks out and blot dry. They should be damp but not dripping.

Cover the working area with newspaper.

 Folk Art Projects • North America EMC 724

▶ Steps to Follow:

1. Take four cornhusks and lay them on top of each other so the edges all meet at the top. Tie them securely at the top with a narrow strip of cornhusk.

2. Flip two of the husks over the tied knot so the knot is now inside. Tie off husks one inch down to form the head.

3. Take one more cornhusk and roll it into a long tube.

4. Slide it up between the four cornhusks to the tie forming the head. This forms the arms. Tie the arms off at each end.

5. Tie the doll around the middle forming the waist. This also holds the arms in place.

   At this point the doll can become a male or female. Leave the husks loose below the waist for a female.

6. Separate the husks into two legs for a male. Tie them closed at the knees and ankles.

   The doll will dry hard in two days.

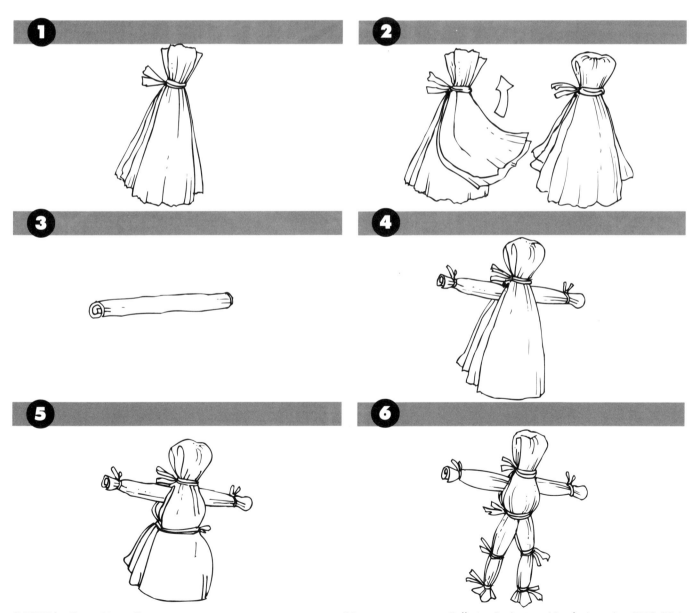

▶ Variations:

Make the shoulders wider by laying flat, wide husk strips over each shoulder like two pieces of a shawl that cross in the front and back. Tie at the waist.

Details can be added using the damp husks. You can add hair, an apron, a head scarf or any details you choose.

Hair - thin damp strips of cornhusk can be braided or rolled around a pencil and allowed to dry to make curls.

Head scarf - wrap thin strips around the head and tie at the neck.

Apron - fold strips of cornhusk over the tie at the waist.

▶ Suggestion:

This activity is much easier if completed with a partner. One person can hold the doll while the other ties.

Navajo Sand Painting
Native American

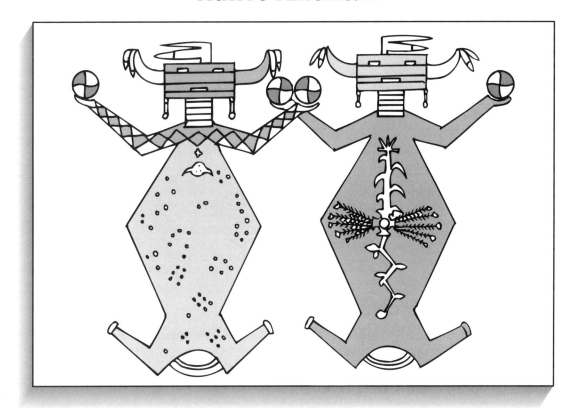

Sand painting is a very ancient Southwest Indian art. Hatals, or chants, are the major Navajo celebrations. The Hatali, or medicine man, leads the singing and makes offerings, such as sacred corn pollen sprinkled in the wind. The medicine man also creates sacred sand paintings. They must be made after sunrise and destroyed before sundown, or made after sundown and destroyed before sunrise. The purposes of sand painting were to evoke healing, rain, safety, or beauty.

Literature Connections:

How the Stars Fell into the Sky: a Navajo Legend by Jerrie Oughton; Houghton Mifflin, 1992.

Ma'ii and Cousin Horned Toad: A Traditional Navajo Story retold by Shonto Begay; Scholastic, 1992.

Navajo Bird Tales told by Hosteen Clah Chee to Franc Johnson Newcomb; Theosophical Publishing House, 1970.

Tapestries in Sand: The Spirit of Indian Sand Painting by David Villasenor; Naturegraph, 1966.

Make a Navajo Sand Painting

▶ **Materials:**

- 1 piece of fairly fine (100) grain sandpaper
- 1 pattern from pages 56-58
- pencil
- carbon paper
- white glue in a squeeze bottle
- colored sand (recipe below)
- paper towel
- newspaper

▶ **Preparation:**

Colored Sand Recipe

In a sealable plastic bag, mix:
- 1 capful rubbing alcohol
- a good squirt of food coloring
- one cup of sand

Zip the bag closed and shake up the sand until it is evenly coated with color. Pour the sand out onto newspaper to dry.

▶ **Steps to Follow:**

1. Transfer the chosen pattern to the sandpaper.

   Lay a sheet of carbon paper on the sandpaper, then lay the pattern on top of that. Press firmly with a pencil and trace over all the lines of the pattern.

2. Decide what color each section will be. You might want to color the pattern with crayon first and use it as a guide.

   Carefully fill in all areas that will be one particular color with white glue.

3. Sprinkle colored sand onto the white glue. Allow the glue to sit for 15 minutes. Then carefully shake the excess sand off onto a paper towel or newspaper.

4. Follow steps 2 and 3 for each color in the design.

 Folk Art Projects • North America EMC 724

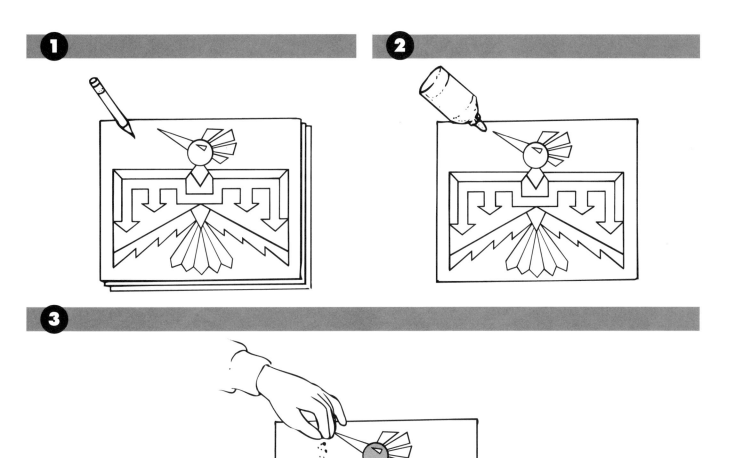

▶ Variations:

Use salt, pepper, and paprika instead of colored sand.

Allow students to create their own design.

Choose a Navajo tale and create a simple pattern to represent its theme.

▶ Suggestions:

If time allows, glue only one color a day. Allow that color to dry overnight before gluing another color.

The patterns can also be used as coloring sheets with younger students.

Folk Art Projects • North America EMC 724

Folk Art Projects • North America EMC 724

58

Mexican Tin Art
Mexico and Central America

Tin was used by humans as early as the Bronze Age. Because it is so soft it can be rolled, pressed, or hammered into extremely thin sheets (tin foil). Mexican tin art is still very popular today and dates back in Mexican history to the 1500s. Candlesticks, plates, frames, and other household objects are made from this popular metal and are often hand painted in bright colors.

Literature Connections:

The Bird Who Cleans the World: And Other Mayan Fables by Victor Montejo; Curbstone, 1991.

The Bossy Gallito: A Traditional Cuban Folktale by Lucia M. Gonzalez; Scholastic, 1994.

Children of the Yucatan by Frank Staub; Carolrhoda Books, 1996.

The Rooster Who Went to His Uncle's Wedding: A Latin American Folk tale retold by Kathleen Kuchers; Putnam, 1992.

Make a Mexican Tin Rooster

▶ Materials:

- Pattern on page 62
- 1 aluminum pie plate (use plates that have a smooth bottom)
- pencil
- scissors
- paper clips
- stapler
- markers (water color markers will work, but permanent markers will be brighter)

▶ Preparation:

The sides of the pie plate need to be cut away. This step should be completed for the younger students before proceeding.

▶ Steps to Follow:

1. Cut away the sides of the pie plate. Save the sides to be used later to make a stand.

2. Cut out the rooster pattern and lay it on top of the round pie plate bottom. Use paper clips to hold it in place.

   Trace over all the lines pressing firmly with a pencil.

3. Remove the paper pattern. Cut away the extra aluminum around the rooster, saving the larger pieces.

4. Using the wing pattern from page 62, trace and cut three wings from the extra aluminum pieces.

5. Color the rooster with marking pens. Water color markers tend to bead up, but if you rub the color a little with your finger, the foil will tint slightly.

6. Attach the wings with staples beginning with the bottom wing first and overlapping the other two.

7. Take the side piece you saved and overlap the ends. Staple it together for a stand.

8. Staple the rooster to the stand.

   Folk Art Projects • North America EMC 724

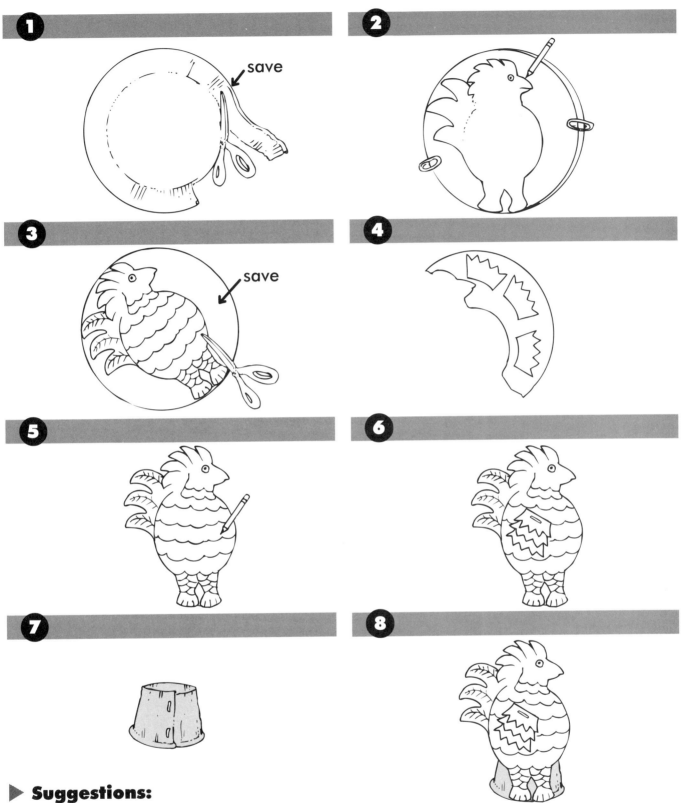

▶ Suggestions:

This project will be difficult for younger students. An adult will need to complete much of the project for them.

Because the foil is thin, it can easily be bent. Encourage students to keep it as flat as possible.

Older students may want to add more intricate designs.

Guatemalan Pottery Plates
Mexico and Central America

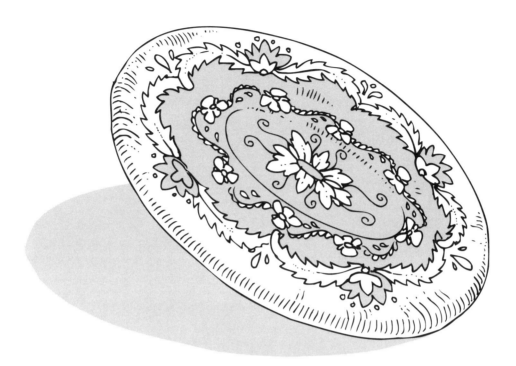

Guatemala, a small country in Central America, is about the same size as Tennessee. It is bordered by the Pacific Ocean, the Caribbean Sea, and also by the countries of Mexico, Belize, Honduras, and El Salvador. Much of northern Guatemala is rain forest. The people traditionally depict the rich colors and sights around them in their pottery. Plates are glazed with bright designs in colors of green, yellow, brown, and blue.

Literature Connections:

Guatemala Is My Home (My Home Country Series); Gareth Stevens, Inc., 1992.
The Hummingbird King: A Guatemala Legend by Argentina Palacios; Troll, 1993.
Nature's Green Umbrella by Gail Gibbons; Morrow Junior Books, 1994.
One Day in the Tropical Rain Forest by Jean C. George; Morrow Junior Books, 1994.

Make a Guatemalan Plate

▶ Materials:

- 1 paper plate
- patterns from pages 66-68
- glue
- scissors
- hole punch
- coloring crayons or markers
- yarn

▶ Preparation:

Begin by photocopying the plate patterns on pages 66-68. You may want younger students to only color one. Older students may color two: one for the front and one for the back of the plate.

▶ Steps to Follow:

1. Students should color pattern designs brightly using mostly green, yellow, brown, and blue.

2. Cut around plate design.

3. Glue to the center of a paper plate.

4. Color edges of plate to blend in with the design.

   Punch a hole in the top of the plate.

   Loop a piece of yarn through the hole to hang.

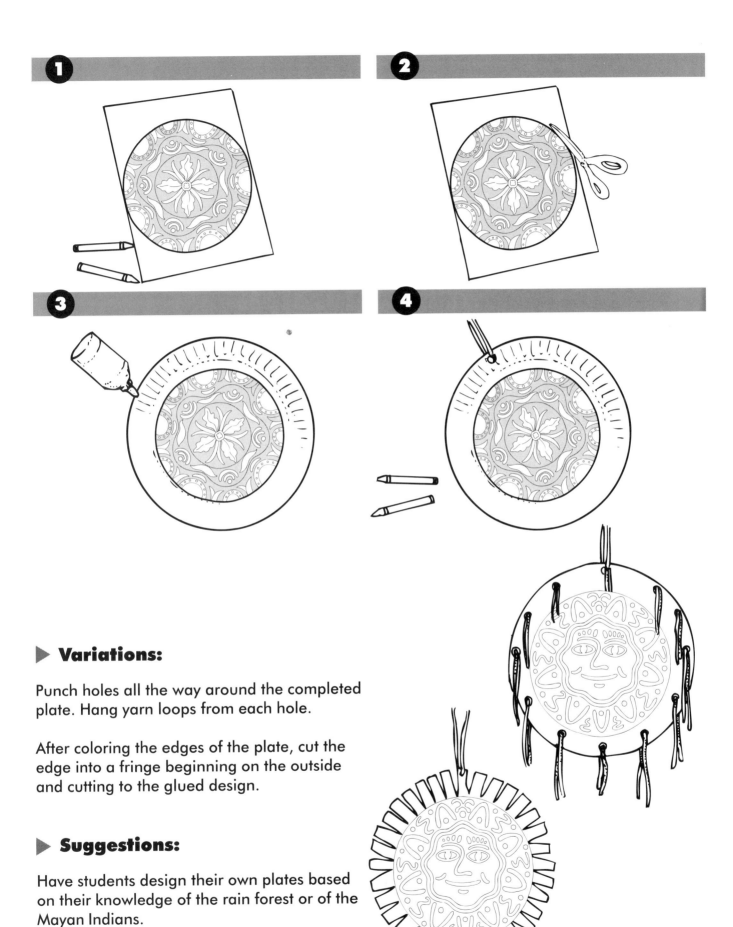

▶ Variations:

Punch holes all the way around the completed plate. Hang yarn loops from each hole.

After coloring the edges of the plate, cut the edge into a fringe beginning on the outside and cutting to the glued design.

▶ Suggestions:

Have students design their own plates based on their knowledge of the rain forest or of the Mayan Indians.

65

66

Folk Art Projects • North America EMC 724

Huichol Yarn Art
Mexico and Central America

People all over the world buy the yarn paintings of the Huichol (WEE-chol) Indians of Northwest Mexico. They are not only beautiful to look at, with brilliant colors and interesting designs, but they also tell stories about the history and religion of the people. An original yarn painting is made by pressing yarn into beeswax that has been warmed by the sun.

Literature Connections:

Gift from a Sheep: The Story of How Wool Is Made by Alberta Eiseman; Atheneum, 1979.
Fiesta! Mexico's Great Celebrations by Elizabeth Silverthorne; Millbrook, 1992.
The Tree That Rains: The Flood Myth of the Huichol Indians of Mexico by Emery and Durga Bernhard; Holiday House, 1994.
Twenty-Five Mixtec Cats by Matthew Gollub; Tambourine Books, 1993.

Make a Yarn Hanging Picture

▶ Materials:

- patterns from pages 72-74
- yarn, many colors
- corrugated cardboard cut
  8 1/2" x 11" (21.5 x 28 cm)
- white glue
- craft stick
- pencil

▶ Preparation:

Demonstrate for students how to use a craft stick to push the yarn into place. If they get glue on their fingers, they should wash their hands immediately. This will keep the yarn from sticking to their fingers and fraying. The craft stick should also be rinsed when necessary.

▶ Directions for Hanging Picture:

1. Glue the pattern to the piece of cardboard. This will provide you with a sturdy base to build your picture.

2. Squeeze glue along a small section of a line on the pattern.

   Take the end of a length of yarn and press it into the glue using a craft stick.

   Continue until the pattern line is covered. Trim any excess yarn with scissors.

3. Cover all lines on the pattern in the same manner. Let the glue dry.

4. Begin to fill in the areas between the pattern lines. Follow the contour of the lines wherever possible.

   Switch colors frequently. Always apply each row of yarn right to next the layer just glued down, so no paper is showing.

5. Continue until you fill up the whole surface of the cardboard with yarn, including the background.

   Let it dry completely.

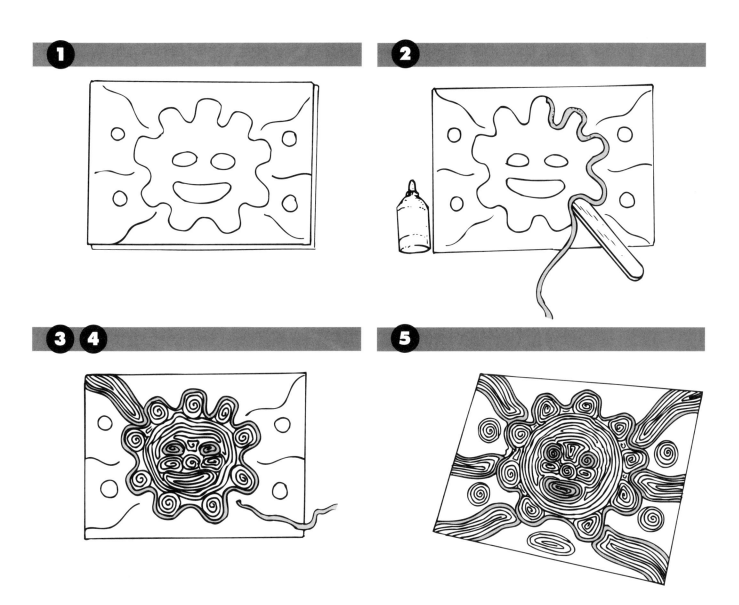

▶ Variations:

Let students make up their own designs. They should sketch lightly with pencil on the cardboard and then follow the steps outlined above.

▶ Suggestions:

Tape a piece of yarn on the back of the pictures so they can be hung.

Younger students can use roving, a thicker yarn. You may want them to cover the pattern lines only.

Older students can use thinner yarn for the more detailed projects.

 Folk Art Projects • North America EMC 724

72

73

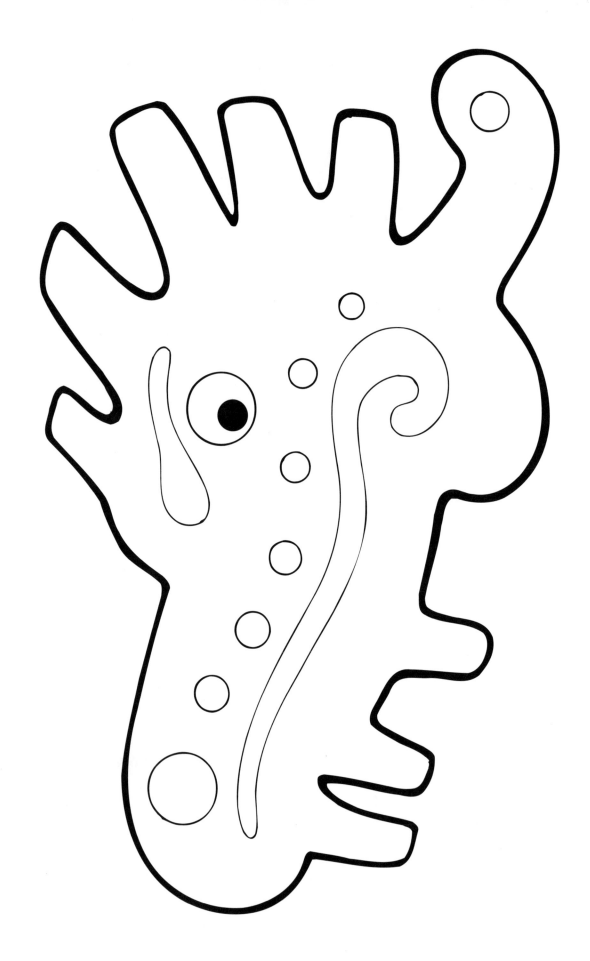

Molas

Molas, cut-through applique, are a beautifully unique craft created by the women of the San Blas Islands off the coast of Panama. The appliqued fabric was originally used in the making of women's clothing. Because the work is so intricate and impressive, panels of it are now being framed and displayed as pictures. The design is created by cutting through layers of brightly colored cotton cloth to show the various colors underneath it. The edges of the shapes are notched, turned under, and sewn down by hand. It is a very exacting and time-consuming job.

Literature Connections:

Indian Folk Tales from Coast to Coast by Jessie Marsh; Council of Indian Education, 1978.
Indian Legends by Johanna R. Lyback; Tipi Press, 1994.
Panama in Pictures from the Series Visual Geography; The Company, 1987.

Make a Paper Mola

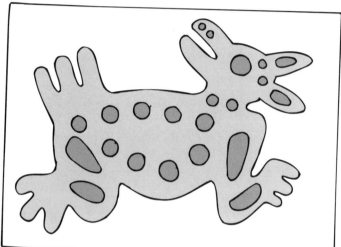

Steps to Follow:

1. Decide how you want to layer the three pieces of construction paper. The directions will refer to them as the top color (the one facing you), the middle color (the one you can't see), and the bottom color (the one at the bottom of the stack).

2. Carefully cut around the outside of the pattern piece and lightly trace it with a pencil on to the top color. Save the pattern piece.

3. Push the point of your scissors into the center of the colored paper and start cutting. Cut carefully. Discard the cut out portion.

4. Cut out the inside design on the pattern piece you saved.

5. Lay the top cut-out colored paper over the middle paper. Then lay the pattern piece in the cut out portion of the top paper.

6. Trace the inside designs onto the middle paper. You may now discard the original pattern piece.

7. Using the tips of your scissors, carefully cut through the designs traced on the middle piece of paper.

8. Glue the three layers together, carefully matching edges.

▶ **Variations:**

Students can design their own paper molas using very simple designs.

For older students, more layers of paper may be added.

Substitute felt for construction paper. The felt may be glued with fabric glue or the students can stitch the felt in place.

Folk Art Projects • North America EMC 724

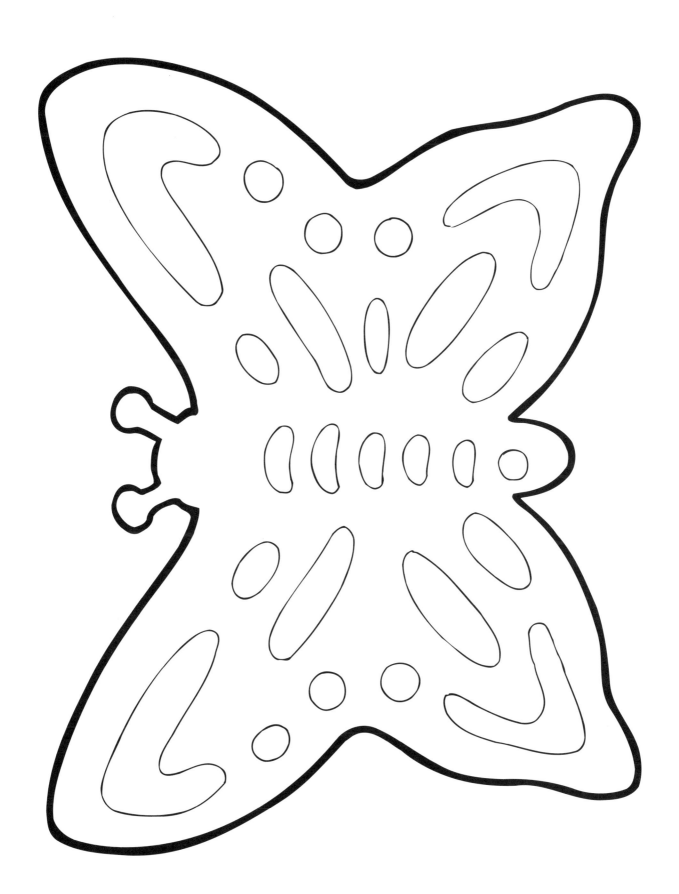

79

Index

Art projects are indexed by type of materials used, by type of art form, and by subject.